The Scout Membership Badge and The Scout Award

Written by
Peter Rogers and Peter Brown

Edited by
Mike Brennan and Stephen Nixey

Illustrated by
Ivan Hissey

Copyright © 1993
The Scout Association
Baden-Powell House, Queen's Gate, London SW7 5JS
ISBN 0 85165 262 X
Reprinted 1994

Welcome!

Whether you have just joined the Scout Troop from Cub Scouts or are completely new to Scouting, welcome!

This book will help you with your training, which is an important part of Scouting, and will help you take a full part in all the exciting games and activities. As you go through the Troop you will gain awards which you will wear as badges on your uniform - and you will be helped by the Scouts in your Patrol and especially by your Patrol Leader.

Awards and badges

The first badge you will work towards is the Scout Membership Badge, which every Scout must gain to become a full member of the Troop. The badge is quite simple and you should gain it quite quickly.

After gaining your Scout Membership Badge you will start on the main Training Programme. This programme is made up of four Awards: the Scout Award; the Pathfinder Award; the Explorer Award; and the Chief Scout's Award. There is one book and badge for each new Award as you progress through the Troop.

Another badge you might want to have a go at, with your Patrol, is the Patrol Activity Award. There are also over 70 Proficiency Badges to try for, so if you have a special interest or hobby there is probably a badge you could get quite easily.

This book contains all the requirements of the Scout Membership Badge, the Scout Award and the Patrol Activity Award. More help with the Patrol Activity Award can be found in the book, *The Patrol Activity Award and the Leadership Award* and all the Proficiency Badges are in the book, *Scout Proficiency Badges.*

Have fun!

The Scout Membership Badge

TO GAIN THE SCOUT MEMBERSHIP BADGE YOU MUST BE AT LEAST TEN YEARS OLD AND MUST COMPLETE EACH SECTION OF THIS BADGE:

1. Talk with your future Patrol Leader about joining the Troop. *(see page 5)*

2. Join a Patrol of your liking and get to know the other members by taking part in an activity with them. *(see page 5)*

3. Get to know the other Scouts and Leaders in the Troop by taking part in at least three Troop Meetings, one of which should be out of doors. *(see page 6)*

4. Show a general knowledge of the Scout Movement and the development of world-wide Scouting. *(see page 7)*

5. Know, understand and accept the Scout Promise and Law. Talk with a Scout Leader about how you can put them into practice each day. *(see page 10)*

6. Know what to do at your Investiture and, if you would like to, invite someone to be there. *(see page 12)*

The Scout Membership Badge is passed under arrangements made jointly by the Scout Leader and the Patrol Leader, and is awarded by the Patrol Leaders' Council.

1

Talk with your future Patrol Leader about joining the Troop.

When you talk with your future Patrol Leader, do not be afraid to ask any questions about what you will be doing with the Patrol and the Troop. Your Patrol Leader will almost certainly want to know what you are good at, so you can be involved in the Patrol right from the start.

2

Join a Patrol of your liking and get to know the other members by taking part in an activity with them.

Everyone in your Troop is keen that you should enjoy yourself and settle in to your Patrol as quickly as possible.

This part of the Award gives you the chance to say which Patrol, or Patrols, you would like to join. It may not be possible for you to join your first choice Patrol, it may have too many Scouts already, but you should be happy with the one you finally join.

This Award requirement says that you should take part in an activity with your Patrol and that could be anything you like. There are some ideas for activities on the next page. If you are unsure of which Patrol to join why not try an activity with each of them to help you make up your mind!

The Scout Membership Badge

Get to know the other Scouts and Leaders in the Troop by taking part in at least three Troop Meetings, one of which should be out of doors.

Illustrated here are some ideas for Patrol and Troop activities.
There are 18 in all. Can you find them all?
(Answers on page 12)

The Scout Membership Badge

4

Show a general knowledge of the Scout Movement and the development of world-wide Scouting.

The Scout Movement was started by a man called Robert Stephenson Smyth Baden-Powell (B.-P.). He was known as Stephe by his family and as a boy he enjoyed pretending to be a hunter or an Indian scout. He attended Charterhouse School and one of his favourite places there was called The Copse. It was out of bounds to all the boys - but avoiding his teachers made it all the more exciting!

With his older brothers, Stephe went on all sorts of expeditions, often on the water. They bought old boats and used them to explore the coast of Great Britain. When they were not on the water, they were learning to look after themselves as they walked for miles with their gear on their backs.

When he left school B.-P. went into the Army and travelled extensively in India and South Africa. In 1888 he was fighting in South Africa and having captured Chief Dinizulu, B.-P. was given a long necklace of wooden beads by him.

Much later on B.-P. used the beads to make the first Wood Badge, which is an Award given to Scouters when they complete their Leadership Training. Look to see if any of your Leaders are wearing their Wood Badge beads.

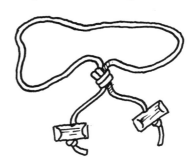

While he was still in South Africa, B.-P. became famous for his defence of a small town called **Mafeking** (now known as Mafikeng). He used all his cunning to hold out against the Boers who outnumbered his men by nine to one. After seven long months, food and supplies became very short. There were so few soldiers that boys from the age of nine upwards worked as messengers on bicycles. Help finally came.

Back in Britain everyone was glad to hear the news that Mafeking had been relieved and agreed that B.-P. was a national hero.

B.-P. was only 43 years old when he became the youngest Major-General in the British Army. He came home to Britain where he found that many boys in the big towns had nothing to do except get into mischief. He decided to put into practice some of the ideas he had used in South Africa for boys in Britain.

Scouting for Boys

He knew that boys enjoyed the outdoor life and so he organised a camp for a group of 20 boys on **Brownsea Island** in Poole Harbour in Dorset. Here he taught them about exploring, camping, boating, stalking, life-saving and many of the things which Scouts still do today. An important principle of the camp was that the boys were 'on their honour' and were trusted to organise themselves, which B.-P. knew they could do.

After the camp, B.-P. completed his book *Scouting for Boys*, which was bought by thousands of boys all over the country. They formed themselves into Patrols and did many of the things they read about in the book. Before long, they found adults to help them and Scout Troops began.

In 1910, B.-P. retired from the Army so that he could give more time to the organisation and development of the new Movement.

In 1920, at Olympia in London, the first international **Jamboree** was held. Towards the end a young Scout declared, 'We, the Scouts of the world, salute you, Sir Robert Baden-Powell, Chief Scout of the World.'

Training Leaders

In order to train adults to become Scout Leaders, B.-P. used a camp site in Epping Forest called **Gilwell Park.** It is still used for training and as a camp site today and is visited by many thousands of Scouts from all over the world each year. B.-P. chose to be known as **Lord Baden-Powell of Gilwell** when he was made a Baron in 1929, and in that same year he was awarded the rare and distinguished Order of Merit of Hungary.

When B.-P. died in 1941, Lord Somers became Chief Scout. Since then, Lord Rowallan, Lord Maclean, Sir William Gladstone, Major-General Michael Walsh and Mr. W. Garth Morrison have all held this appointment.

The Scout Membership Badge

Development of World-wide Scouting

That first camp on Brownsea Island for 20 young people, together with the book *Scouting for Boys*, proved to have great appeal for young people across the world. Since that first camp Scouting has never stopped growing and is now enjoyed by over 16 million Members in more than 150 countries and territories.

As a result of Baden-Powell taking a holiday in South America, Chile was one of the first countries outside of the United Kingdom to begin Scouting. At much the same time (1910) Scouting also became established in the USA and Canada. And so it grew! Many of its recent Members come from developing countries and from countries now politically free to operate Scouting - such as countries in central and eastern Europe, like Russia and the Ukraine.

Scouting has doubled its Membership world-wide in the last 20 years, and it is estimated that more than 250 million people have been Scouts!

Most Scouts around the world have been invested in a similar way to the way you will be invested here in the United Kingdom and many of them receive the same World Membership Badge. Receiving the Membership Badge is the first step to being an active Member of this great world-wide Movement.

The Scout Membership Badge

5

Know, understand and accept the Scout Promise and Law. Talk with a Scout Leader about how you can put them into practice each day.

THE SCOUT PROMISE

*On my honour,
I promise that I will do my best to do my duty to God and to The Queen, to help other people and to keep the Scout Law.*

Depending on your faith and on which country you come from there are different versions of the Scout Promise you can make to help it suit you. If you are in any doubt about this ask your Scout Leader.

THE SCOUT LAW

1. A Scout is to be trusted.
2. A Scout is loyal.
3. A Scout is friendly and considerate.
4. A Scout belongs to the world-wide family of Scouts.
5. A Scout has courage in all difficulties.
6. A Scout makes good use of time and is careful of possessions and property.
7. A Scout has self-respect and respect for others.

There is something about the Scout Movement which makes it different from most other youth organisations. Like most of these organisations there are plenty of activities, but before you can be a Scout you have to make a promise. When you are invested as a Scout, part of the ceremony will be to make the Scout Promise and the rest of the Troop will be listening, so you had better mean it!

On my honour, I promise that I will do my best ...

You begin by telling everyone that on your honour (which means 'what I am saying is very important to me') that you will 'do your best'. A promise is something that you should always try your hardest to keep. No one expects you always to succeed, but you will know when you are doing your best.

to do my duty to God and to The Queen ...

A duty is something that you have to do. Life is much more enjoyable if you choose to do things before someone tells you that you have to.

Many people believe that our world only makes sense if there is a God, although they all understand God in different ways. As you get older, your 'duty to God' should become clearer as you find out more about yourself and other people and by talking, listening and reading about your faith.

Your duty to the Queen includes showing respect for her and for the country. At flag break we salute the Union flag to show this - but it should not stop there. Our country has laws which we should obey and help others to keep as well.

to help other people ...

Scouts are always keen to help others. When you see a need, get in first and find out if you can help. And remember - a good turn does not really count if you expect a reward for it.

and to keep the Scout Law.

If you look through the Scout Law you will not find 'A Scout is always brainy' or 'A Scout is a brilliant athlete' but you will find things which any Scout really can do.

1. A Scout is to be trusted.

If you say you will do something, make sure you do it. When people know they can trust you they will give you far more important and interesting things to do.

2. A Scout is loyal.

Loyalty means choosing something and sticking to it. In what ways can you show you are loyal to your Troop and to your friends?

3. A Scout is friendly and considerate.

Most people like to have lots of friends. Good friends are often made by sharing and sometimes thinking about what they would like rather than what you want. Scouts are also considerate to people they do not know - by not making noise at night which could wake young children or by not leaving a trail of litter wherever they go, for example.

4. A Scout belongs to the world-wide family of Scouts.

There is a special sort of friendship between Scouts, not just in your own Troop, but everywhere. On many Scout camp sites you can see this 'family' atmosphere as Scouts from different areas share things.

5. A Scout has courage in all difficulties.

This is another chance to do 'your best' when things start to get tough. It takes real courage to stick at something no matter how difficult it becomes.

6. A Scout makes good use of time and is careful of possessions and property.

How do you use the time after you get home from school? Do you get down to homework or look after your pets or do you go straight out and join your friends? You must plan your time to fit in everything you want to do. Sometimes you must sort out what is most important and do that first.

Are you just as careful about other people's things as you are about your own? A Scout looks after things without having to be told to, which means they will always be there the next time you want to enjoy them.

7. A Scout has self-respect and respect for others.

As you get older you need to learn to look after yourself. At camp, there may not be someone who will tell you off if you do not wash for a week, but the distance everyone keeps away from you might make you change your ways! Keeping fit and healthy is a good way of showing respect for yourself.

You need to respect your mind as well. Learn as much as you can and try to understand the world around you. That includes listening to other people's points of view and respecting their opinions even when you disagree.

6

**Know what to do at
your Investiture and, if you
would like to, invite someone
to be there.**

Investiture

When you have completed the
requirements of the Scout Membership
Badge and feel ready to make your
Promise you will be invested as a
Scout. 'Invested' is the formal word for
joining. Your Investiture is an important
occasion because you are about to
make a very important promise, so
before that night you need to be sure
exactly what is going to happen.

Investitures are slightly different in
every Troop, but you will probably stand
out in front of the Troop with your Patrol
Leader and make your Promise. The
Scout Leader may check with you that
you understand the Promise and Law
and that you know what honour means.
You may also have the Troop flag,
called the colours, lowered in front of
you and be asked to put your hand on it
when you make your Promise.

When you have made your Promise you
will probably be given some badges by
your Scout Leader and your Patrol
Badge by your Patrol Leader. Ask your
Patrol Leader exactly how things are
done in your Troop.

Inviting someone

Making your Promise is quite a serious
decision as there is no point in making
promises if you are not going to keep
them! If you read the Scout Promise
and Scout Law again you will find that
there is quite a lot that you are being
asked to do.

Because it is such an important
promise, you may want to ask someone
to come along with you to hear you
make it. This might be a good friend or
a parent. Once you have made your
Promise, hopefully this person will help
you keep to it.

Only when the Scout Promise is being
said is the Scout Sign used.

Good luck!

Answers (from page 6):

*Archery; Ballista construction; Candle cooking; Dry slope skiing;
Forestry; Horse riding; Igloo construction; Joinery; Kite making;
Model railways; Night hike; Rafting; Subaqua; Trampolining;
Underground exploration; Windsurfing; Xerographic art; Yachting.*

The Scout Award

Congratulations on passing your Scout Membership Badge and joining the world-wide Scout Movement. The next badge you will be doing is the Scout Award which is open to all Scouts aged 10½ - 11½ years old.

Most of the requirements for the Scout Award are grouped into one of these six sections: Scoutcraft; Adventure; Culture; Community; Health; Commitment. All of the progressive training Awards in the Scout Training Programme contain these sections with the same titles to help you find your way around.

Many of your Patrol and Troop activities will include bits from more than one section. Air and Sea Scouts will find many opportunities to take part in air and water activities which will count towards the Scout Award.

You will also have to complete part of the Patrol Activity Award and gain a Proficiency Badge. There are Proficiency Badges on over 70 subjects. If you are particularly interested in air or water activities, there are Airmanship and Seamanship Proficiency Badges as well.

Scoutcraft

Many of the skills in this section are the basic training you need to be able to take part in Scouting activities. These include camping, cooking, first aid and navigation skills.

Adventure

The Adventure section covers a huge range of activities - hikes, camps, visits, expeditions - and a whole lot more.

As you begin to take part in more adventurous activities you need to learn how to do things safely. Your first taste of camping may well be with your Patrol or Troop, when older Scouts will show you how to look after yourself.

Culture

The Culture section looks at creative things you can take part in. This might be in entertain-ment, a show or music, art, drama or playing an instrument. The list is endless!

Community

It's so easy to take things for granted, such as telephones, public transport and the emergency services. But we all depend on each other, and part of your training is to see how the complex world in which we live operates.

Health

If you want to enjoy Scouting to the full you will need to be fit and healthy. Plenty of exercise, good food and hygiene all help.

Commitment

A lot of what you do in Scouts is great fun, but you will also be expected to think seriously about things at times. Commitment means sticking at things and this section will help you do it.

How to succeed

Activities

Scouting involves a wide variety of activities - camping, hiking, first aid, cooking - and many Troops also go canoeing, rock climbing, gliding, sailing and lots more. During these activities you may complete a part of the Award you are working for, and this book will tell you just what to do for each part.

If you do the same activity with a minimum of three others from your Patrol, you may also complete part of the Patrol Activity Award - two for the price of one!

Planning

You do not have to work through each part of the Award in the order they are printed.

Most parts of the Awards can be done at any time. Others are best done at certain times of the year - such as expeditions in the summer - and some can only be done after you have completed some training.

Many of the requirements can be completed in camp - especially a long camp - or during a Patrol or Troop Meeting. Some will take several weeks and will need careful planning.

Safety

As you get older you will probably want to go on more adventurous activities so you must start learning now how to make sure things are as safe as possible for everyone involved. Accidents can easily spoil the fun and adventure - always be on the lookout for ways to stop them happening. Build safety into your training until it becomes second nature.

Scouts with special needs

If you have a disability or a particular difficulty which you feel might stop you from completing an activity, have a word with your Scout Leader. The Patrol Leaders' Council is responsible for making sure you have a fair chance to gain all the Awards and they have the authority to make changes to the programme if necessary. They should also make sure that you can join in all the activities and do not have to miss out for any reason.

Why not find a friend and work on your Scout Award together?

For Scouts aged 10½ - 11½

To be passed under arrangements made by a Patrol Leader and awarded by the Patrol Leaders' Council.

HOLD THE SCOUT MEMBERSHIP BADGE. SUCCESSFULLY COMPLETE ALL OF THE FOLLOWING:

Scoutcraft

1. Pitch, strike and store a tent correctly. *(see page 16)*
2. Prepare, cook, serve and clear away a meal and a hot drink out of doors using an open fire. *(see page 18)*
3. Be familiar with safety precautions for the correct use of potentially dangerous equipment such as lamps, stoves, axes and saws. *(see page 21)*
4. Be able to perform mouth-to-mouth ventilation and demonstrate the recovery position. Know how to deal with shock, fainting, nosebleeds, stings, minor cuts, burns and scalds. *(see page 22)*
5. Complete a simple navigation exercise involving map and compass. *(see page 26)*
6. Demonstrate the correct use of six knots, bends or hitches used in Scouting activities. *(see page 28)*
7. Pack a rucsac to include provisions, clothing, first aid kit, map and compass for a weekend camp. *(see page 30)*

Adventure

8. With suitable equipment, complete a one-day expedition with friends by foot, bicycle, canoe or sailing dinghy. *(see page 31)*
9. Camp for two nights. *(see page 32)*

Culture

10. Make an active contribution to an entertainment, show or exhibition. *(see page 34)*

Community

11. Know the location of, and be able to give directions to, local facilities such as telephone boxes, police station, bus and railway stations, public toilets; know how to call out emergency services. *(see page 35)*

Health

12. Improve your personal performance over a period of one month in an activity such as jogging, aerobics, Scout pace, circuit training, swimming and keep a simple record of your performance. *(see page 37)*

Commitment

13. Explain to your Patrol Leader (or Scout Leader) how the Scout Promise and Law are relevant to your daily life. *(see page 39)*

From the Patrol Activity Award

14. Take part in a meeting of the Patrol-in-Council. *(see page 40)*
15. Take part in an outdoor Patrol activity. *(see page 40)*

From the Proficiency Badge Scheme

16. Gain one Proficiency Badge. *(see page 42)*

The Scout Award Requirements

Scoutcraft

Pitch, strike and store a tent correctly.

Every tent is different and has its own best way of being **pitched** (put up) and **struck** (taken down) but here are some general points which will help if you ever have to pitch a tent which is new to you.

• As you unpack the tent note how it is folded and what bits go in which bag - this will help with packing it up.

• Find a suitable piece of ground - flat, with no sharp objects - and peg the groundsheet out. Check that the door of the tent does not face into the wind and that you like the view!

• Fit the poles together and attach them to the tent. For large tents with wooden poles they probably go inside; for small tents with metal poles they probably go outside the tent but under the flysheet. Watch out for any metal spikes which might tear the material.

• Use two or three other Scouts to hold the tent upright over the groundsheet while you put the largest pegs in place for the main guy-ropes. Once these are tight your helpers should be able to let go and help you put the rest of the pegs in:

− set the corner guy-ropes at right angles to each other (pegs following the line of the guys).

− other guy-ropes in line with the seams in the canvas (pegs in line too!).

− brailing pegs (corners first, pulling the walls tight).

− pegs should go into the ground at an angle of 45 degrees and the guy-ropes should pull on them at right angles.

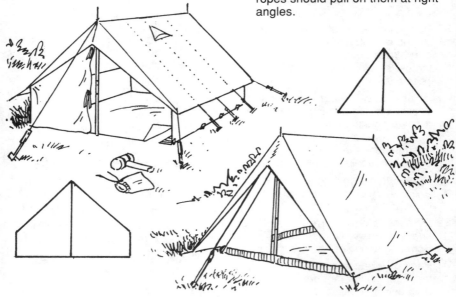

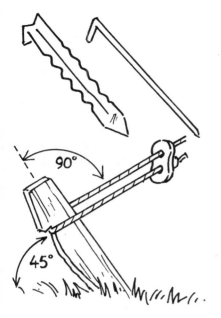

everyone will be happy and the tents will last much longer. A good Scout is not someone who thinks that camping is 'roughing it' but one who knows how to be comfortable in camp.

Comfort includes keeping dry and warm and your tent will only keep out the rain and wind if it stays waterproof and does not get torn.

• Keep everything (and everyone) from rubbing against the inside of a tent in the rain or water will come through.

• Never walk on the tent while you are pitching it or striking it as this will take the waterproofing off and may damage the canvas.

• Pitch it correctly. This way the canvas will not be under strain. If the tent looks well pitched (everything neatly in line and nothing sagging) then it probably is!

• Always pack the tent away dry. If not, it will rot very quickly and be ruined. If you have to strike camp in the rain, always spread the tent out to dry as soon as you get home, ideally by hanging it up if possible.

• Always clean the pegs. Even when they are put into a separate bag, mud dries and then gets everywhere. Clean the pegs by scraping one peg with another and leave them spread out to dry.

• Always count the number of pegs so that you know you have not left any behind.

• Adjust all the guy-ropes until the material of the tent is pulled just tight enough to look smooth and not sag.

Once your Patrol has mastered the way to pitch your tent, try these activities:

• Try pitching a tent you have never pitched before.

• Pitch a tent with everyone blindfolded except the Patrol Leader.

• Record the time it takes to pitch your tent and then see if you can beat this time without being careless, which might cause damage.

• Make up a scrapbook of tents: use pictures from catalogues, describe each tent you have used and so on.

Tent care

Your tent is your home and in camp it needs looking after if you are going to enjoy living in it. An active Patrol in a good Troop uses its tents so often that the few simple rules about tents are quickly learned. If you stick to them

2

Prepare, cook, serve and clear away a meal and a hot drink out of doors using an open fire.

Before you start, collect plenty of wood of different sizes. You will need dry **kindling** to get the fire started - dead leaves, paper, birch bark and so on. These will not burn for long and you must use the heat from them to make the wood catch fire - thin twigs first, which will in turn help to light the bigger stuff.

Decide where to light the fire - well away from tents, trees and hedges which might also catch fire.

You do not want the grass catching fire, so lift enough turf (about eight centimetres thick so the roots are not destroyed) to give a patch of bare ground for the fire with a good gap around it. Keep the turf in a cool damp place so that you can put it back when you have finished.

If you are using a farmer's land check first before lifting the turf. Landowners may prefer you not to turf as animals can sometimes dig the fire up later. Always take the farmer's advice.

If the turf must be kept for more than a day or two, store it upside down with the roots on the top and keep it well watered.

The fire needs to be built carefully - don't just pile on lots of wood and hope for the best!

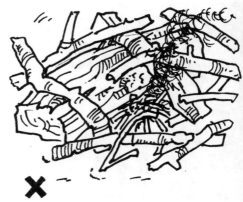

For the wood and kindling to burn they need oxygen (which is in the air) but too much wind can blow out a small flame. Watch the fire carefully and shield it from strong winds. Blow gently to help the flames to spread.

Once the fire is alight, put a few larger pieces of wood at the end of it where the wind blows the flames on to them. When they are well alight, add more wood to the other end. The fire will be hottest and best for cooking when the wood has burnt for a while and has red and glowing embers rather than flames. When you add more wood aim to keep at least one part of the fire just right for cooking on.

Cooking

Here are some ideas for simple meals and drinks.

Sausages can be put onto a peeled stick and held over glowing embers or cooked with a little fat in a frying pan together with eggs, bacon, mushrooms, tomatoes and onions. If using a stick make sure it is not holly, elm or yew which are poisonous!

Twists are made using a stiff dough of flour and water. But first you need to find a thin green stick.

Peel the bark off and then heat the stick over the fire before you wind the dough around it. When it is cooked, the twist should slide cleanly off the stick. Add jam and it's delicious!

Potatoes can be baked in foil in the glowing embers which are left after the flames have died down. Bananas and apples as a dessert can also be cooked this way.

Pancakes are made from batter which should be made about two hours before you need it. To make about eight pancakes you will need an egg, a mugful of flour, a pinch of salt, a mugful of milk and a little fat.

Put the flour and salt in the bowl and make a well in the centre.

Drop the egg and half the milk into the well and stir gradually until all the flour is mixed in. Try to make sure the mixture is smooth with no lumps, then slowly add the rest of the milk, beating all the time.

Put a tiny amount of fat into a frying pan and wait until it is really hot. Tilt the pan so that it is evenly coated with fat. Pour just enough batter into the pan to cover the bottom with a thin layer. As the pancake cooks through, it should come unstuck from the pan and you can then turn it over to cook the other side.

Serve with lemon and sugar.

After your meal you might like to try twists for fun.

Do not forget you have not finished until the fire is put out and levelled, the turf put back and all the washing up done!

3

Be familiar with safety precautions for the correct use of potentially dangerous equipment such as lamps, stoves, axes and saws.

Unless you have been camping with the Cub Scouts or with your family, much of the equipment you will use in the Scouts will be new to you, tents, lamps, axes, saws, portable toilets and so on.

Unfortunately many of these items, if used wrongly, can be dangerous. Nearly everything that is used in creating heat and light (including fires) requires some kind of fuel and can burn you. This part of the award is to help you to understand the dangers so that you can help prevent accidents to yourself and to others.

Lamps and stoves

Every Scout Troop will have different types of lamps and stoves, some perhaps many years old, and each will have its own instructions on how to use it which must be followed.

All lamps and stoves use some type of burning fuel and this is usually the dangerous bit. They might use:

- Petrol
- Methylated Spirits
- Paraffin
- Gas
- Solid fuel tablets

Petrol, methylated spirits and paraffin all burn easily. They should always be stored in sealed, clearly marked containers and never be left anywhere near a naked flame or fire. When these are heated they also give off vapour, which burns just as easily, so that even though you can see no liquid left it can still burst into flames.

Gas usually comes in pressurised containers, either small sealed cans that the lamp or cooker will puncture, or in larger bottles with a tap. Gas also burns very easily and should never be left anywhere near a fire as it may well explode.

Here are a few safety rules to remember:

- Always follow the manufacturer's instructions carefully.

- If there are no instructions ask for help - never guess.

- Always keep fuels away from naked flames, lights and fires.

- Never try to refill a hot lamp or stove as the vapour may light or even explode.

- Never throw a gas or fuel container on a fire even though you think it is empty - it still might explode.

- Never play with fuels.

To help you with this part of the Award why not ask the Scout Leader or Quartermaster to give you a safety display of your Group's equipment? You are not expected to remember how everything works at this stage but you must understand the safety rules.

Why not hold a quiz afterwards to see how much everyone remembers?

More information on stoves can be found in the book *Enjoy Camping*.

Scoutcraft

Axes and saws

As part of your Pathfinder Award (the next badge) you might choose to demonstrate how to use axes, knives and saws, but for the moment all you need to know are the safety rules.

Axes, knives, saws and spikes are all usually very sharp - they would not be of any use if they weren't! Like anything else that's sharp, they are potentially dangerous if not used properly. The safety rules, therefore, are very simple:

- Do not try to use something you haven't been trained to use.

- Never play with sharp tools - they are not toys.

- Always **mask** (cover up) the blade when not in use.

- Always carry a blade correctly (see below).

- Always put tools away in a safe place when not in use.

Most Groups will have the equipment talked about here, but check with your Scout Leader or Quartermaster what other potentially dangerous equipment there is. You might, for example, ask why it can be dangerous filling a portable toilet - just see what answer you get!

4

Be able to perform mouth-to-mouth ventilation and demonstrate the recovery position. Know how to deal with shock, fainting, nosebleeds, stings, minor cuts, burns and scalds.

First aid means knowing what to do when you find that an accident has happened - how to stop the situation getting worse, how to get help and how to treat a casualty until help arrives. Much of what you need to know is plain common sense, but it has to be taken seriously and learnt properly.

To help you remember the important things there is a simple code to follow:

D - check out **danger.**

O - make the right **observations.**

T - set to work on the **treatment.**

Danger

If you arrive on the scene of an accident, the first thing you must do is make sure the emergency services are called, then help to prevent the situation getting worse and stop further accidents happening.

• At a road accident, check that someone is directing traffic.

• If someone has been electrocuted, do not touch them until the source of the shock has been removed or the power has been switched off.

• Where an accident involves a burning building or something which might collapse, carefully move everyone out of danger as long as you will not be in danger - do not become a casualty yourself!

You should not move any injured person unless there is some danger - you could make their injuries worse. Wait until expert help arrives.

Make a list now of different places where accidents happen. What danger must you look out for in each place?

Observation

When you want to find out what is wrong you do not only use your eyes - you need to listen carefully to everything the injured person and any bystanders say. While you are doing this, reassure everyone involved by telling them that help is on its way. If casualties are conscious, talk to them, comfort them and carry out, as far as their injuries allow, the treatment for shock. Watch for any changes in their condition which you can report when help arrives.

Treatment

If someone has stopped breathing then you have about three minutes in which to get oxygen back into the bloodstream before there is a risk of permanent brain damage - or even death.

Mouth-to-mouth ventilation

Clear the mouth of any loose objects, for example seaweed, false or broken teeth, chewing gum. Make sure the tongue is free of the airway.

Tilt the head back, pinch the nose tightly to prevent air escaping and, after taking a deep breath, blow firmly into the mouth.

As you blow, watch the chest rising, then move your mouth well away so that you may breathe in a new supply of fresh air.

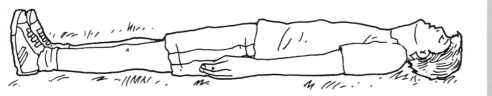

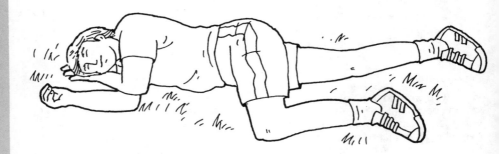

Do not pause during the first four inflations. After that, wait for the chest to fall each time before blowing again. A good guide to the correct breathing rate is to breathe out and then count to yourself 'one thousand, two thousand, three thousand', then breathe out again, and so on. It is important, however, that whenever you practise mouth-to-mouth ventilation you should use a purpose-built model, and **never** someone who is already breathing.

Recovery position

If someone is unconscious and breathing then they should be put in the **recovery position** which will help them breathe and prevent them from choking (see above).

Learn the correct way to put someone into the recovery position and then practise with members of your Patrol.

Shock

There are many different things that can cause shock. If someone is involved in an accident or loses a lot of body fluids or blood, they can suffer from 'traumatic' shock. The skin becomes

pale, cold and clammy and the person will feel weak, faint and giddy. They might also feel sick or start yawning, sighing or perhaps start sweating a lot.

Reassure the casualty and make them comfortable. Raise their legs slightly unless you think there could be a fracture. Keep them warm with a blanket or coat. Loosen any tight clothing. All the time, talk to the casualty; tell them what you are doing. Do not move them unnecessarily as this will increase shock.

Never give the casualty anything to eat or drink (it might cause problems if a hospital needs to give an anaesthetic). If they are really thirsty you can wet their lips with water which should help.

Never let the casualty smoke or drink alcohol.

Fainting

If someone is standing up for a long time, such as in school assembly, they can faint due to a drop in the flow of blood to the brain. The symptoms are very similar to those of shock.

If someone simply feels faint, it may be enough to let them sit down. Help them to lean forward with their head between their knees and tell them to take deep breaths.

Do not give a person anything to eat or drink until fully conscious, and then only sips of cold water.

Nosebleeds

The biggest danger with a nosebleed is that the casualty might swallow too much blood or breathe it in. To help prevent this you should:

• Sit the person down with the head well forward and loosen any tight clothing around the neck.

• Tell him to breathe through his mouth and to pinch the soft part of his nose.

• Ask him to spit out any blood that gets into his mouth.

• After about ten minutes, release the pressure and, if the bleeding continues, pinch for another ten minutes.

• If bleeding continues, seek help from a doctor or hospital.

• Once the bleeding has stopped tell the casualty to take it easy for a while and not to blow his nose for at least four hours.

Stings

Some people are allergic to certain types of sting and will need to go to hospital if they are stung, but usually stings only cause local swelling and a sharp pain.

If the sting from an insect has been left behind, it should be carefully removed using tweezers.

To stop the pain and swelling you can put on a cold compress (such as a towel or clean handkerchief soaked in cold water), surgical spirit or a solution of bicarbonate of soda.

Minor cuts

The danger with any cut is that germs might get in and cause infection. So:

• Wash your hands before you start.

• Carefully clean the wound under running water or using a piece of wet cotton wool with antiseptic. Wipe away from the wound - you do not want to push dirt into it.

• Dry the wound by dabbing it gently.

• Choose a sticking plaster which is big enough to cover the wound, peel back the plastic strips and put the plaster on without touching the sterile gauze in the middle.

Burns and scalds

If an injury is caused by 'wet heat' for example steam, hot water, fat or any hot liquid, it is called a **scald.** An injury caused by 'dry heat' such as a fire or hot surface is called a **burn**.

The treatment is the same for both:

• Reassure the casualty.

• Place the injured part quickly under running cold water, or immerse it in cold water for at least ten minutes or until the pain has gone.

• Gently remove any rings, watches, belts, shoes and so on as appropriate before any swelling starts.

• Cover with sterile, non-fluffy material.

Never remove any burnt clothing that has stuck to the wound.

Never use sticking plasters.

Never put any creams, ointments or fat on the injury.

Never burst any blisters.

If in doubt, with all first aid seek professional medical help.

5

Complete a simple navigation exercise involving map and compass.

You could do this as part of Troop Night or during an outdoor Patrol Meeting. A map is really just a picture of what the ground looks like from directly above, with North at the top of the map. Details like roads, hills and some buildings are marked by special symbols, which you will usually find on the **key** at the edge of the map.

Navigation exercises

Find a map of your area and see if you can find your own house, school and Scout Headquarters on it. The best map to use is an Ordnance Survey 1:50 000 which has a scale of two centimetres to one kilometre. Follow the roads and paths you usually take to get to school or to Scouts and work out all of the features you pass on the way.

Use the same map to plan a route which you have never been on before - out into the countryside if possible.

Work out what the map says you will pass on the way and then go and check. A map on its own is useful only if you can see some landmarks which you can use to find out where you are on the map.

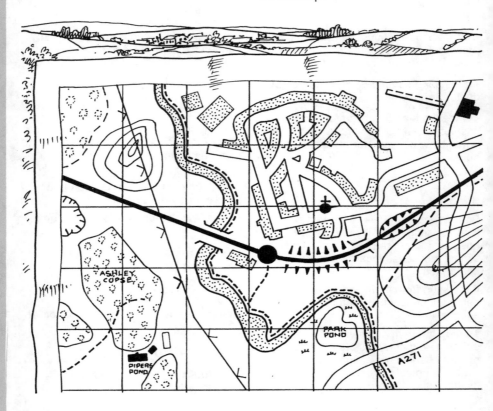

Setting a map

To set a map you simply turn it round so that whatever is in front of you in real life is in front of you on the map. Choose two easy land marks like a church and a railway station and check they are on the left or right as they should be. If not, turn the map round. When they are in the right place as you are looking at them the map is set.

Compass

Once you begin to go into unknown countryside, perhaps onto moors where there are few landmarks anyway, you need to be able to rely on using a compass accurately.

Begin by learning the names of the main points of the compass and use them. For this exercise you need only use your compass for general direction checks, but if you want to know more detail ask your Patrol Leader to show you how to set the map using the compass.

Why not have a Patrol competition in which your Patrol Leader asks you questions based on a local map, and you have to use the map to find the answer? Or two Patrols could give each

other sealed instructions for how to get to a mystery destination, using compass directions and map features. That's a test of your route planning skills as well as your navigation!

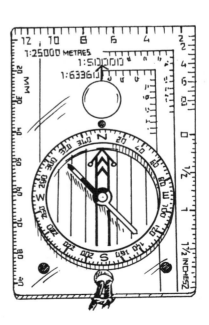

6

Demonstrate the correct use of six knots, bends or hitches used in Scouting activities.

Even though you have only been in the Troop for a short time you will already have come across at least one knot, the reef knot. How can I be so sure? Well, like every other Scout, you are wearing it. It is on your purple World Badge!

Knots, bends and hitches are used a lot in Scouting activities, both in making things like swings, bridges, gadgets and so on and in adventurous activities such as climbing, abseiling (going down a cliff, usually backwards) and sailing. Most people given two bits of rope could tie them together somehow, but could they be sure that the knot would hold them together? Could they be sure it would not slip if they were climbing down a cliff and their life depended on it?

The reason we learn knots is so we can do a job quickly and efficiently and know that the knot will do what we want it to do, so we can be sure it will be safe.

The different names, knot, bend or hitch in years gone by had very specific meanings but these have changed greatly over the years. Basically, a **knot** is a complication in a rope of some kind, usually in one rope. A **bend** ties two rope ends together (usually different ropes) and a **hitch** ties the rope to another object.

Here are a few knots, bends and hitches for you to try but there are many, many more. If you are a Sea Scout or think you would enjoy sailing why not try and find six that are particularly used on boats or ships. If you have been a Cub Scout you will already know some of the following knots, so try to learn some new ones.

Granny Knot
a knot to be avoided

Thief Knot —
useless just a catch

Surgeon's Knot —
the extra hitch prevents slip

A knot for tying a rope to a post, spar or ring etc. is called a Hitch.

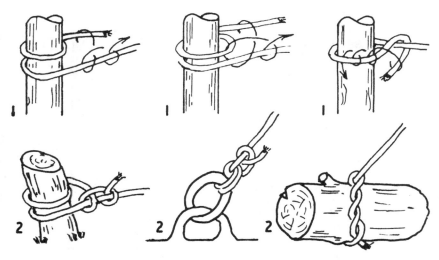

Round Turn and Two
Half Hitches

Fisherman's
Bend
also **Anchor Hitch**

Timber Hitch

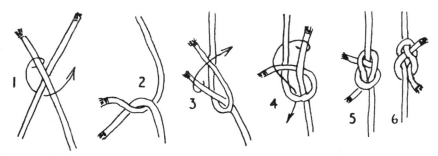

Sheet Bend

7

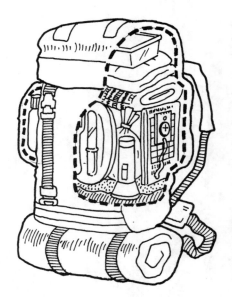

Pack a rucsac to include provisions, clothing, first aid kit, map and compass for a weekend camp.

A rucsac is an expensive piece of equipment but once you have decided that you enjoy Scouting it is worth getting a rucsac that will last well. Look at the different types that other Scouts have, ask your Leaders about them and remember that whatever you choose, it is you who will have to carry it, maybe over many kilometres of rough country. Biggest might not be best!

A good way of deciding what you will need for a weekend camp is to think through the programme step by step and put things out on your bed as you think of them. If you try to pack them all in your rucsac straight away you will probably end up unpacking it all again just to check you have got everything!

So start your thinking on Friday night and think 'I'll probably go in uniform so when I get there I'll need to change into . . . and then at night I'll need . . . and in the morning . . . and when we go on activities . . . '

When you've got all your personal equipment, not forgetting your torch, map, compass, plates and so on have a go at packing your bag and seeing if you can lift it. If it will not all go in or if it's too heavy, go through it again and see what you can leave out.

Think carefully about the order in which you pack things.

• Put in first what you will need to use last (spare clothing, swimwear, etc.).

• Put large items in and then pack smaller ones around them.

• Keep things you will need and 'emergency' items handy - pack them last or in separate pockets (map and compass, first aid kit, waterproofs etc.).

• Don't put hard objects where they will dig into your back (plates, mug, cutlery etc.).

• Wrap things in polythene bags to keep them dry (but make sure the bags never blow away at camp).

• Fold clothes carefully, then fold them again to make them as small as possible.

• Don't let Mum or Dad do all the packing for you - you'll never get it all in again to come home!

8

With suitable equipment, complete a one-day expedition with friends, by foot, bicycle, canoe or sailing dinghy.

Where you choose to go for your expedition is really up to you, but it should be a real adventure that helps you practise the skills of navigation, packing equipment and cooking that you have already gained from this Award. What you will take with you depends on how you travel but it might include:

Map or chart (with waterproof cover)

Compass

Waterproofs

Spare clothes

Whistle

Stove

Fuel

Food

First aid kit

Emergency repair kit

By canoe

If you are travelling by canoe remember:

- Put everything into strong waterproof bags.
- Keep things handy which you will need often like map/chart and compass, waterproofs, spare sweater and so on.
- Don't let anything get round your feet which might prevent you getting out quickly if you need to.

By bicycle

Remember, if travelling by bicycle it is safer and more comfortable to use panniers than to put your things on your back, and don't forget to balance the weight of the panniers. Remember to wear your cycle safety helmet and light coloured clothing at all times when cycling.

By dinghy

Make sure all your equipment is suitably packed in waterproof containers and stowed correctly.

9

Camp for two nights.

The two nights do not have to be together, but the camp must be under canvas.

There are many different reasons why Scouts camp:

• It's fun.

• Tents can be used as somewhere to sleep overnight on a long-distance hike.

• It helps you to learn how to look after yourself, your clothes and your belongings.

• It can give you a base camp for other activities, such as sailing, climbing or gliding.

• You can stay in thousands of places other people can't.

• You can experience living together as a Patrol, which is a very good way to get to know one another better.

First camp

For your first few camps you will find there is much to learn - unlike home, your 'bedroom' is much smaller for instance! Things which seem essential at home you may have to do without;

but there will be so much going on that you will probably hardly notice.

Here are some tips which will make life easier in camp:

• Lay out your sleeping bag as soon as you can and preferably before it gets dark.

• Find out where the toilets are - and check on where toilet paper is kept and where you can wash your hands.

• Remember you are not the only one in the tent; keep your stuff neatly together or put it away in your rucsac. Never walk on a groundsheet in boots or shoes - take them off or kneel down and reach over for what you want.

• When you are using wood fires, you always need plenty of firewood which someone has to fetch so don't always wait to be asked. Don't waste wood by putting it onto a fire when it is not needed.

• Plan what you are going to do with rubbish. Some can be burnt, greasy water is best strained into a pit through leaves or grass which is burnt and renewed each day. Cans and bottles are best put in a dustbin, or taken home to be thrown away or recycled.

- Keep your eyes open for suitable logs or anything you can use to make seats, tables and other gadgets.

- If the weather turns wet but it is still warm, why not put your swimming trunks on and get out? If you do have to stay in the tent, keep wet coats and boots well away from everything else.

- Never be afraid to ask your Patrol Leader or an older Scout questions about anything - they were new to camping once as well!

What to do in camp

If your camp is simply a base for other activities, you may have decided to take along stoves and fuel to speed things up. Otherwise, you will have to spend some time each day collecting firewood, laying and lighting the fire and preparing and cooking food. If you see all this as part of camping you will enjoy it every bit as much as the games and other activities. Work with a friend and you can talk and joke as well - but remember you have a job to do!

When your Patrol Leader tells you there is some free time, use it to:

- Explore the area around the camp site. Find out who else is on the site - you might well discover some new friends.

- Keep your eyes open for any wildlife. Look out for animal tracks and also any unusual plants or trees.

- Make some gadgets, like a washstand or a drainer for the plates and cutlery, or a gateway.

- Whittle a tent-peg or carve a decorative item such as a woggle.

- Make a sundial by putting one stick in the ground then, using a watch for one day, place a stone where the shadow of the stick falls each hour.

- Produce a coloured picture using natural materials - grass, berries, leaves and so on.

- Build an obstacle course and hold a camp sports competition.

- Make and test a boomerang.

Camping with a difference

You could try:

- **Cycle camping;** make sure your bicycle is in good working order and load all your gear into panniers, not on your back.

- **Canoe camping;** you must train properly and make sure you have the right Authorisation if one is needed.

- **Pony trekking;** either as an activity at camp or to take you between camp sites.

10

Make an active contribution to an entertainment, show or exhibition.

We all have some talent and it is important that you discover what yours is - and use it! For some, this will be an individual effort - playing the piano or guitar, displaying some photographs you have taken or reciting a story. For this Award you don't have to stage a mega-show all on your own. An active part in something your Troop or Group or school is doing is alright and you don't have to be a performer.

Presentations which require an active contribution from a number of people include Gang Shows, amateur dramatics, playing in an orchestra or band, or helping put together programmes on local or hospital radio. It is not only those 'in the public eye' whose contribution is important - backstage and other technical roles are just as vital. However, simply to sell programmes on the night is hardly an active contribution - unless that is, you also designed or printed the programmes! Why not put on a Troop show for the parents or do a short entertainment at a regular Group Meeting.

Exhibitions

For an exhibition to be really successful, it needs to be eye catching. Try to think of something original. Visit your local library or museum and see how the exhibitions are arranged. What do you notice first? What can you remember afterwards? Use these good techniques in your own displays. Why not:

• Mount an exhibition of what the Troop or your Patrol does for your Group's fair or annual general meeting?

• Take a series of photographs of local features from unusual angles and mount them around a street map of the area?

• Help to arrange a display of Troop activities which involve Scouts using equipment while people watch - perhaps as part of a parents' evening?

• As part of a gymnastics team or Scout Band, make an active contribution to a public display?

11

Know the location of, and be able to give directions to, local facilities such as telephone boxes, police station, bus and railway stations, public toilets; know how to call out emergency services.

Copy out the chart and fill in where the nearest telephone boxes, police station and so on are to be found.

Other facilities may include:

Post box
Doctor
Dentist
Hospital
Vet
Town Hall
Library
Museum
Swimming baths
Sports complex

Petrol station
Post office
Newspaper offices
Local radio station
Theatre
Cinema
Scout Shop
Chemist
Supermarket
Fish and chip shop
Launderette
Places of worship
Coastguard station
Mountain rescue service

and anything else in your area which a stranger might ask the way to. You might also mark them on a map of the area.

Directing strangers

If someone asks you the way to one of these places, think clearly about the best route. Remember that a motorist cannot take the short cut through a back alley which you might be able to do on foot!

Try to give the names of landmarks which they should pass - like shops, churches and other large buildings. Try not to use road names (which can be

	Near to home	Near to Troop meeting place
Telephone box		
Police station		
Bus station		
Railway station		
Public toilets		

difficult for a driver to see) but give some idea how far it is from one landmark to the next - and whether it will be on the left or right.

Never get into a stranger's car.

Young people have been attacked by strangers who suggested they get into their cars.

Emergency services

In most places the fire brigade, police and ambulance can be called out by dialing 999 from any telephone. Even from a public call box these calls are free. In some areas you can also contact the coastguard or mountain rescue service in this way.

A 999 call is given top priority and is obviously not to be used except in a real emergency.

When the operator asks you 'Which service do you require?' you should say 'Fire', 'Police', 'Ambulance' or whichever service you want. You will

also have to tell the operator the telephone number you are calling from. Once you are connected to the service you asked for, state:

• Briefly, what has happened;

• Where it is;

• How many people are involved;

• Your own name.

Wait until the officer you are speaking to tells you they have all the information they need.

12

Improve your personal performance over a period of one month in an activity such as jogging, aerobics, Scout pace, circuit training, swimming and keep a simple record of your performance.

Do you keep yourself fit? There are so many different ways to keep fit that it should not be hard to find one you enjoy.

Exercise helps because it:

- Keeps your heart and lungs in good condition;
- Keeps your neck, back and joints supple;

- Gives you strength;
- Makes you feel good, in mind as well as body. And if that is not enough - it can be great fun too!

How fit are you?

Here are two simple tests to find out how much **stamina** you have - that means how long you can keep going.

Climbing stairs

For this test you need some stairs - about 15 steps. Walk up and down them, fairly quickly, three times. After you have finished, you should be able to hold a conversation without being at all out of breath.

Step-ups

Find a strong chair or a firm bench and step up onto it with both feet and then down again. Change which foot goes up first each time - left then right, and so on. Stop as soon as you get out of breath. If this is after less than three minutes, then you definitely need more exercise!

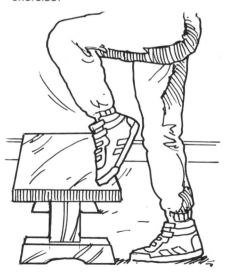

S-factor scores

	stamina	suppleness	strength
Badminton	★★	★★★	★★
Canoeing	★★★	★★	★★★
Climbing stairs	★★★	★	★★
Cricket	★	★★	★
Cycling	★★★★	★★	★★★
Disco dancing	★★★	★★★★	★
Football	★★★	★★★	★★★
Gymnastics	★★	★★★★	★★★
Hill walking	★★★	★	★★
Jogging	★★★★	★★	★★
Judo	★★	★★★★	★★
Rowing	★★★★	★★	★★★★
Sailing	★	★★	★★
Squash	★★★	★★★	★★
Swimming	★★★★	★★★★	★★★★
Tennis	★★	★★★	★★
Walking (briskly)	★★	★	★
Weightlifting	★	★	★★★★

The S-factors

Stamina Is only one of the three important S-factors. Exercise also helps to improve your **suppleness** - that is how much you can bend or twist, which is important to prevent aches and pains or pulled muscles.

The third factor is **strength** - and this comes from various sorts of exercise, as the table above shows.

These are just a few of the activities you could choose. **Scout pace** is a special kind of running and walking - you run for 50 paces and then walk the next 50 paces, run 50 more and so on.

Getting started

Once you have decided which activity you will do, here are some ideas which may help:

• Get together with another Scout and then compare your progress each Troop Night.

• Ask your P.E. teacher to help, particularly if several Scouts in your Troop go to the same school.

• Get Mum or Dad involved - see who improves most during the first month!

• Set yourself a sensible target based on how good you are at present. For example, if your limit now is to swim six lengths, aim to build up to ten lengths by the end of the month.

You must also keep a simple record of your performance for one month and show an improvement.

13

Explain to your Patrol Leader (or Scout Leader) how the Scout Promise and Law are relevant to your daily life.

Do you remember when you were invested? You repeated the Scout Promise in front of the Troop, and since then you have had to see how well you could keep that Promise. Remember you promised to do your best - that is something everyone can do if they try.

The Scout Promise and Law are not just meant for when you are with Scouts - on Troop Night and at camp. If you really try to use them it should make a difference to your whole life - at school, at home and with your friends.

A Scout in everyday life

Neil Stevens was a pretty ordinary sort of lad. As you read his story, try to see where the Scout Promise and Law come in. Do you think he made a good Scout?

Neil enjoyed life at Hilbury. School wasn't bad and now that he had been a Scout for about six months, he was well on his way to gaining his Scout Award. His favourite subjects at school were Geography and P.E. Whenever they were using the atlas he would turn to the maps which showed the vast unexplored areas of the world and imagine he was leading a party searching for a lost tribe, cutting their way through dangerous jungles and crocodile infested swamps. It was all so real to him that he was given top marks for a story he had written for homework. That really pleased him.

That afternoon, the maths teacher asked Neil if he would go to the stock room to collect some new exercise books. He gave him the key and said which shelf the books were on. Neil unlocked the door and looked in. He stopped for a moment and stared at all the books and calculators and everything. A thought flashed through his mind - they would never notice just one book missing. Neil hesitated and then realised that his teacher had really trusted him with the key. He collected the books and locked up again.

When he told his friends later how he could have helped himself to anything he wanted, they laughed at him and told him he was stupid. Only Sue stuck up for him and said he had done the right thing. Sue was also a Scout, but in a different Troop from Neil. They were always talking about what their Troops did, whose was the best, and how they were both going to win the District Camping Competition.

Neil was finding one thing really tough. His parents insisted that he went to church with them, even though he didn't really want to go. Only last week, he told his Dad, a mate of his had said it was all rubbish anyway. 'You should wait until you can make up your own mind,' his Dad told him, but meanwhile he would be going to church. He listened to his father and then went to get ready. First he carefully packed away the models he had been working on. His Mum never seemed to see where he had put things on the floor, so it was safer to pick them all up. He would come back to them later.

How have you done in putting your Scout Promise and Law into action?

39

FROM THE
PATROL ACTIVITY AWARD

14

Take part in a meeting of the Patrol-in-Council.

15

Take part in an outdoor Patrol activity.

For this Award, the Patrol Activity must involve at least four Scouts from the same Patrol working together. This may include the Patrol Leader and the Assistant Patrol Leader.

The full requirements for the Patrol Activity Award are given on page 41 and in the book, *The Patrol Activity Award and the Leadership Award.* You can be working for this Award at the same time as the Scout Award. If activities are done with at least three other members of your Patrol some may even count for both!

Your Patrol

To work together as a Patrol you need to get to know one another and find out what you like doing.

It is important that you join in with your Patrol as much as possible. When Patrol Meetings and activities are arranged, make a note of them and tell your parents so that they don't go and organise something else for you to go to.

Patrol-in-Council

The Patrol-in-Council is simply the name given to the time you meet together with your Patrol. Your Patrol will meet together to discuss activities, good turns, and anything which concerns you as a Patrol. You might also be asked what Award choices you would like to do next. At this Patrol-in-Council meeting, the Patrol Leader will probably be in charge, but everyone is allowed to have their say.

The meeting itself should not be too formal, but try not to get distracted too often and start discussing last night's television or whatever!

Outdoor Patrol activities

For this part of the Scout Award, you will be expected to take an active part in an outdoor activity with a Patrol. You might get together one evening, or for an afternoon one weekend, or during the holidays. The list of possible activities is endless, but here are a few suggestions.

• Cooking: have a go at making pancakes over an open fire.

• Tents: pitch a Patrol tent and hold your meeting inside it.

• Pioneering: practise building some camp gadgets.

• Tree identification: visit a local park and see how many types of tree you can name. You could make a survey by counting the number of each type or draw a map of the park to show them.

• The Scout Award: include some of these activities in your Patrol meeting. That way you can pass both at the same time!

The full requirements of the Patrol Activity Award are as follows:

1. Be in a Patrol of your liking.

2. Explain the Patrol system.

3. Show a knowledge of your Patrol name.

4. Take part in three meetings of the Patrol-in-Council.

5. Take part in a Patrol Good Turn.

6. Complete four of the following activities:

   a. Take part in an indoor Patrol Meeting.

   b. Take part in an outdoor Patrol Meeting.

   c. Take part in a joint Patrol activity (within your own Troop, or with a Patrol from another Troop or a Guide Company).

   d. Take part in a Patrol exchange with another Troop or Guide Company.

   e. Take part in a short Patrol camp (for example, a weekend).

   f. Take part in a Patrol expedition (for example, a weekend).

   g. Gain a Collective Achievement Proficiency Badge.

   h. Any other one activity of a similar nature and level of achievement as agreed with the Patrol Leaders' Council.

Gain one Proficiency Badge.

You can work for Proficiency Badges at the same time as the other awards. There are over 70 to choose from - decide now which ones you are going to try to get.

To give you some idea here are some of the badges with brief details of what you have to do. Full details of each badge are in the book *Scout Proficiency Badges*, which is available from your local Scout Shop.

If you are a Sea Scout or an Air Scout, you may choose to gain a Seamanship or Airmanship Proficiency Badge.

Athlete

You have to compete in any three events, at least one of which must be a track event and one a field event. You will gain points depending on how good you are. To complete the badge successfully you must get a minimum number of points which depends on how old you are.

If you already have the 3 Star Award of the British Athletics Federation, you qualify for the badge automatically.

Camp Cook

The cooking has to be done under camp conditions and preferably on a wood fire. There are several parts to this badge, including:

- Cooking without utensils - using foil;
- Making a cooked breakfast and serving it properly;
- Cooking and serving a main course and a sweet;
- Planning two menus, including quantities, for a Patrol.

Camper

This badge requires you to have a good knowledge of how to camp well. This includes:

- Knowing how to pitch and strike various tents;
- Choosing a good site to camp;
- Understanding camp hygiene - cleanliness, waste disposal and so on;
- Showing how to store food and fuel correctly;
- Making camp gadgets;
- Cooking a hot meal.

Cyclist

Your bike must be properly equipped and in good working order. You will be expected to know how to make simple adjustments and repairs - like mending a puncture, replacing a brake block or adjusting the height of the saddle.

You must read *The Highway Code* and know about traffic signals, lighting-up times, road signs and be able to read road maps - which means knowing about road numbers like A405, B692 and so on.

Finally, you have to take part in a Scout activity which uses bicycles, not forgetting you should always wear a cycle helmet. If you have passed the National Cycling Proficiency Test you will automatically pass some parts of this badge.

Swimmer

You will have to show you can do all of the following:

• Swim 200 metres using any stroke; use two more strokes to swim 50 metres in each one.

• Perform a standing dive from the side of the bath.

• Know how to use simple rescue methods.

• Recover an object which is under two metres of water.

These are just some examples. Remember, the full list of the requirements for each badge is in the book, *Scout Proficiency Badges.*

Finished? - Congratulations!

When you think you've finished all the requirements of this Award check through them with your Patrol Leader. If everything is done ask your Patrol Leader to raise the matter at the next Patrol Leaders' Council so that you can get your Award.

If you are 11½ years old and have not quite finished your Scout Award, don't worry. If you want to finish it then have a word with your Scout Leader. If not then move on to the Pathfinder Award.

Good luck with your Pathfinder Award!

Notes

Notes

Notes

Notes